Anna's Prayer

For Annie and Kimberly

Special thanks to James and Bonnie Parkin for their invaluable input

Leatherwood Press LLC
8160 South Highland Drive
Sandy, Utah 84093
www.leatherwoodpress.com
Text Copyright © 2008 Karl Beckstrand
Illustrations Copyright © 2008 Shari Griffiths

ISBN 978-1-59992-113-6
Printed in the United States.

Anna's Prayer

Written by Karl Beckstrand

Illustrated by Shari Griffiths

ANNA MATILDA ANDERSON was a young girl who lived in Sweden in the 1880s. Her family had a two-room house, a tiny plot of ground with fruit trees, and a pretty flower bed. They had a chicken and some rabbits. Because they were poor, Anna's mother had to sell the eggs, apples, and plums—and sometimes a rabbit—in the city. Anna and her older sister, Ida, picked beautiful wildflowers to sell for one or two pennies per bunch.

In the summer they enjoyed long days and sunlit nights. But they were very cold during the dark winters, when the sun's visits were short.

When Anna and her family joined The Church of Jesus Christ of Latter-day Saints, people treated them badly. It was very hard for Anna's mother to find work after joining the Church. Even their friends turned against them. Anna and her family had to leave their little home and move to the city.

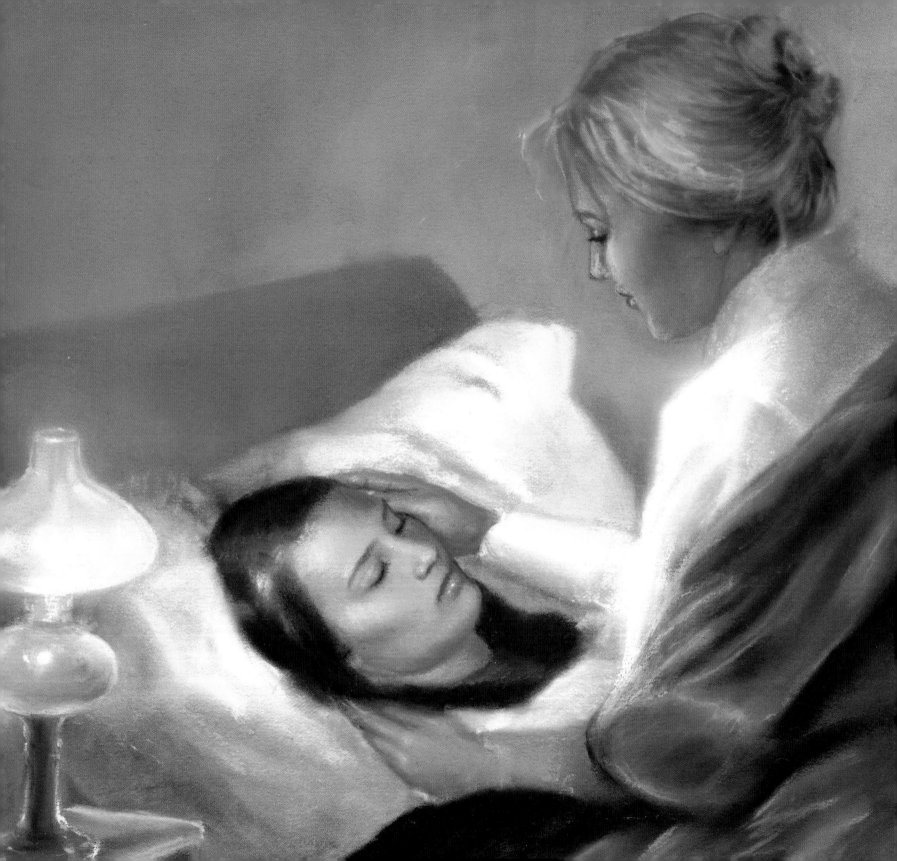

Anna's mother had to work away from home all day and into the night, even when her children were sick. When Ida got scarlet fever and had to stay in the hospital, her mother would walk ten miles to the hospital to visit her, then walk back home again. She made this trip many times. She was a wonderful mother.

When Anna was ten years old, her sister, Ida, was offered a job working for a family in America. They even paid for a boat ticket. Anna's mother wanted Anna to have a better life too. She had just enough money saved to send Anna to live with her aunt in Salt Lake City, Utah. She told Anna how excited she was for her daughters to go to America. "You will learn English and have so many adventures," she said.

Anna and her sister sailed on a big boat for the United States in May 1888. On the dock, Anna's mother wept as she said goodbye to her girls. "These are tears of joy," she told them, wrapping Anna snugly with her own tattered shawl. Anna's tears fell too. Her heart was breaking, and she wondered if she would ever see her mother again.

Once in America, the sisters traveled by train to Ogden, Utah, where Ida headed to her new job in Idaho. Anna was to continue by herself to Salt Lake City, where her aunt was supposed to meet her at the train station.

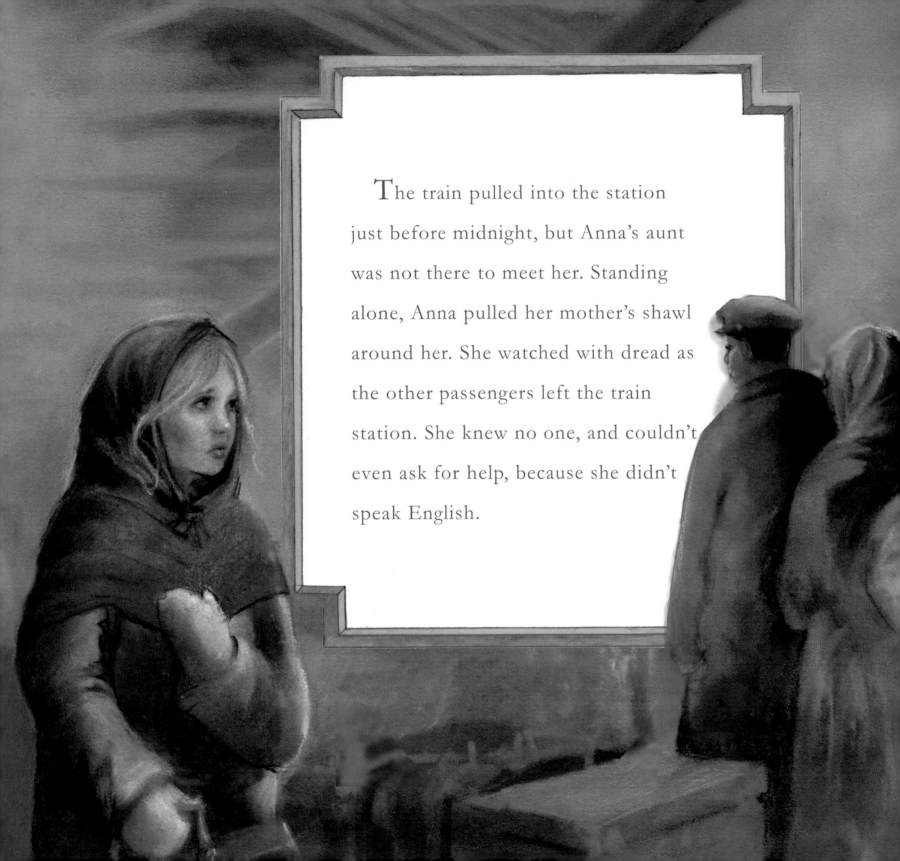

The train pulled into the station just before midnight, but Anna's aunt was not there to meet her. Standing alone, Anna pulled her mother's shawl around her. She watched with dread as the other passengers left the train station. She knew no one, and couldn't even ask for help, because she didn't speak English.

When only one family remained in the station, Anna began to cry. Then she remembered something her mother told her before she left: "If you come to a place where people can't understand you, don't forget to pray to your Father in Heaven. He understands you." Anna knelt by her traveling bag, bowed her head, and pleaded for help. She desperately needed someone who understood and spoke Swedish.

The last family was leaving the station. Seeing Anna's plight, they motioned for her to follow them. Anna followed, clutching her traveling bag. She walked slowly, wondering what would happen to her.

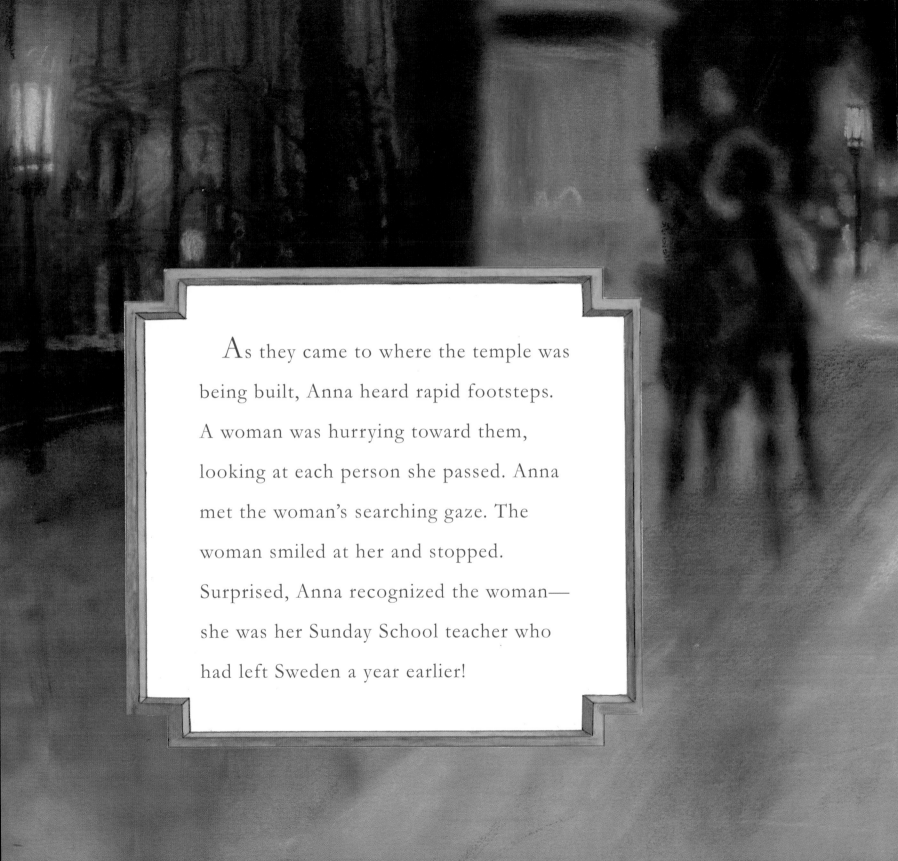

As they came to where the temple was being built, Anna heard rapid footsteps. A woman was hurrying toward them, looking at each person she passed. Anna met the woman's searching gaze. The woman smiled at her and stopped. Surprised, Anna recognized the woman— she was her Sunday School teacher who had left Sweden a year earlier!

Pulling Anna into her arms, the teacher wiped away Anna's tears. Speaking in Swedish, she told Anna, "I was awakened from my sleep over and over. Images of arriving immigrants raced through my mind, and I couldn't go back to sleep. I felt I must come to the temple to see if I knew anyone here."

Anna's Sunday School teacher brought Anna to her own house. Later, Anna was reunited with her aunt, who had not received the letter with Anna's arrival date. Anna and her sister soon had enough money to send to their mother so she could join them in America. How happy they were to be together again!

Anna did learn English. But her Swedish prayer in the train station would forever be a special memory. She had only asked for someone who could understand her, but Heavenly Father sent someone who loved her.

Anna Matilda Anderson was born January 26, 1878, in Björklund, Furingstad, Ostergotland, Sweden. She and her sister, Ida, immigrated to the United States in May 1888. Anna married David Peter Soffe on April 4, 1899, in the Salt Lake Temple. They had six children and eighteen grandchildren. Anna died April 15, 1963, in Bountiful, Utah. She rests alongside her husband in the Salt Lake City Cemetery.

ABOUT THE AUTHOR

Karl Beckstrand is from San Jose, California, and currently resides near Salt Lake City, Utah. He obtained a bachelor's degree in journalism from Brigham Young University and has experience in television, radio, and film. Karl's other titles include *Sounds in the House, Crumbs on the Stairs,* and *Life Is Packed*.

ABOUT THE ILLUSTRATOR

Shari D. Griffiths is a painter and illustrator who loves to paint people and their stories. She graduated from Brigham Young University with a bachelor's degree in illustration. Shari and her husband live in Portland, Oregon, and are expecting their first child. *Anna's Prayer* is Shari's first children's book.